Adoration

30 FAVORITE SONGS OF PRAISE & WORSHIP

EASY TO PLAY
EASY TO SING

Arranged for Piano and Voice by

TERESA WILHELMI

LILLENAS PUBLISHING COMPANY
Kansas City, MO 64141

CONTENTS

Majesty

J. W. H.

JACK W. HAYFORD
Arr. by Teresa Wilhelmi

Stately
slight rall.
a tempo
3
Maj - es - ty, wor - ship His
maj - es - ty. Un - to Je - sus be all glo - ry, hon - or, and
praise. Maj - es - ty, king - dom au -
thor - i - ty Flow from His throne un - to His own; His an - them

raise. So ex - alt, lift up on high the name of
Je - sus. Mag- ni - fy, come glo- ri - fy Christ Je - sus, the King.
Maj - es - ty, wor- ship His maj - es - ty– Je - sus who
died, now glo - ri - fied, King of all kings.
Opt. Fine

So ex - alt, lift up on high the name of Je - sus. Mag- ni - fy, come glo- ri-
slight rit.
Broader, more majestic
fy Christ Je - sus the King. Maj - es - ty,
wor- ship His maj - es - ty–
Je - sus who died, now glo- ri -
fied, King of all kings.

He Has Made Me Glad

L. V. B.

LEONA VON BRETHORST
Arr. by Teresa Wilhelmi

a tempo
rit.
I will en-ter His gates with thanks - giv-ing in my heart; I will
en-ter His courts with praise. I will say, "This is the day that the
Lord has made!" I will re-joice for He has made me glad.
He has made me glad; He has made me glad. I will re-joice for
1
2
He has made me glad. He has made me glad.

Emmanuel

B. McG.

BOB McGEE
Arr. by Teresa Wilhelmi

Em - man - u - el,
us,

Em - man - u - el,
re - vealed in us!

His name is called
His name is called

1

Em - man - u - el: God with

2

Em - man - u - el.

Opt. Fine

Em - man - u - el,
us,
Em - man - u - el,
re - vealed in us!
His name is called
His name is called
1
2
Em - man - u - el:
God with
Em - man - u -
el.

Great Is Thy Faithfulness

THOMAS O. CHISHOLM

WILLIAM M. RUNYAN
Arr. by Teresa Wilhelmi

1. Great is Thy faith - ful - ness, O God, my Fa - ther; There is no shad - ow of turn - ing with Thee. Thou chang - est not; Thy com - pas - sions, they fail not. As Thou hast been Thou for - ev - er wilt be.
2. Sum - mer and win - ter, and spring - time and har - vest, Sun, moon, and stars in their cours - es a - bove, Join with all na - ture in man - i - fold wit - ness To Thy great faith - ful - ness, mer - cy, and love.

Great is Thy faith-ful-ness! Great is Thy faith-ful-ness! Morn-ing by
morn-ing new mer-cies I see. All I have need-ed Thy hand hath pro-
If using the arrangement as a piano solo, omit this repeat.
vid-ed. Great is Thy faith-ful-ness, Lord, un-to me!
Opt. Fine
rit.

a tempo
3. Par - don for sin and a peace that en - dur - eth,
Thy own dear pres - ence to cheer and to guide,
Strength for to - day and bright hope for to - mor - row–
Bless - ings all mine, with ten thou - sand be - side!

Great is Thy faith-ful-ness! Great is Thy faith-ful-ness! Morn-ing by
morn-ing new mer-cies I see. All I have need-ed Thy
hand hath pro-vid-ed. Great is Thy faith-ful-ness, Lord, un-to me!
Opt. tag
rit.

Bless His Holy Name

A. C.

ANDRAE CROUCH
Arr. by Teresa Wilhelmi

Bless the Lord, O my soul, and all that is with - in me, bless His
ho - ly name.
Opt. Fine
Bless the Lord, O my soul, and all that is with - in me, bless His
ho - ly name.
He has done great

things, He has done great things, He has done great
things, bless His ho - ly name. Bless the Lord,
O my soul, and all that is with - in me, bless His ho -
ly name.
rit.

The Bond of Love

O. S.

OTIS SKILLINGS
Arr. by Teresa Wilhelmi

1. Love thro' Christ has bro't us to-geth - er,
Melt - ing our hearts as one. By God's Spir - it
we are u-nit - ed, One thro' His bless - ed Son. We are
one in the bond of love; We are one in the bond of

love. We have joined our spir- its with the Spir - it of God; We are
Opt. Fine
one in the bond of love.
2. Now, dear Lord, we
join in wor - ship; Thank You for all You've done.

Thank You for this love You gave us; Thank You for mak-ing us
one. We are one in the bond of love; We are
one in the bond of love. We have joined our spir-its with the
Spir - it of God; We are one in the bond of love.
rit.

Glorify Thy Name

D. A.

DONNA ADKINS
Arr. by Teresa Wilhelmi

1. Fa - ther, we love You, we wor - ship and a - dore You. Glo - ri - fy Thy
2. Je - sus,
name in all the earth. Glo - ri - fy Thy name,
glo - ri - fy Thy name. Glo - ri - fy Thy name in all the earth.
If using the arrangement as a piano solo, omit this repeat.

rit.
a tempo
3. Spir - it, we love You, we wor - ship and a - dore You.
Glo - ri - fy Thy name in all the earth.
Glo - ri - fy Thy name, glo - ri - fy Thy name.
rit.
Glo - ri - fy Thy name in all the earth.

Come, Thou Fount of Every Blessing

ROBERT ROBINSON, alt.

TRADITIONAL AMERICAN MELODY
Arr. by Teresa Wilhelmi

1. Come, Thou Fount of ev-'ry bless-ing, Tune my heart to sing Thy grace. Streams of
mer-cy, nev-er ceas-ing, Call for songs of loud-est praise. Teach me some me-lo-dious
son-net, Sung by flam-ing tongues a-bove. Praise the mount! I'm fixed up-on it, Mount of
God's un-chang-ing love.

2. O to grace how great a debt - or Dai - ly I'm con - strained to be. Let that
grace, now like a fet - ter, Bind my yield - ed heart to Thee. Let me know Thee in Thy
full - ness; Guide me by Thy might - y hand Till, trans - formed, in Thine own
im - age, In Thy pres - ence I shall stand.
Opt. tag
8va

We Bow Down

T. P.

TWILA PARIS
Arr. by Teresa Wilhelmi

1. You are Lord of cre - a - tion and Lord of my
life, Lord of the land and the sea. You were Lord of the heav - ens be -
fore there was time, And Lord of all lords You will be! We bow
down and we wor - ship You, Lord. We bow down and we wor - ship You,

Opt. Fine
Lord. Lord of all lords You will be!
2. You are King of cre - a - tion and King of my life, King of the land and the
sea. You were King of the heav- ens be - fore there was time, And King of all
kings You will be! We bow down and we crown You the King. We bow
down and we crown You the King. King of all kings You will be!

All Creatures of Our God and King

FRANCIS of ASSISI, tr. by WILLIAM H. DRAPER

From "Geistliche Kirchensesange", 1623

Arr. by Teresa Wilhelmi

1. All creatures of our God and King, Lift up your voice and with us sing: Alleluia! Alleluia! Thou burning sun with golden beam, Thou silver moon with softer gleam, O praise Him! O praise Him! Al-le-
2. Thou rushing wind that art so strong, Ye clouds that sail in heav'n along, O praise Him! Alleluia! Thou rising morn, in praise rejoice; Ye lights of evening, find a voice! O praise Him! O praise Him! Al-le-

If using the arrangement as a piano solo, omit this repeat.
lu - ia! Al - le - lu - ia! Al - le - lu - ia!
lu - ia! Al - le - lu - ia! Al - le - lu - ia!
3. Let all things their Cre - a - tor
bless, And wor - ship Him in hum - ble - ness. O praise Him! Al - le - lu - ia! Praise,
praise the Fa - ther, praise the Son, And praise the Spir - it, Three in One! O praise Him! O
praise Him! Al - le - lu - ia! Al - le - lu - ia! Al - le - lu - ia!
Ped.

Open Our Eyes

R. C.

ROBERT CULL
Arr. by Teresa Wilhelmi

O - pen our eyes, Lord; we want to see Je -
O - pen our ears, Lord, and help us to lis -

sus, To reach out and touch Him,
ten. O - pen our eyes, Lord;

1

and say that we love Him.

2
Opt. fine
we want to see Je - sus.

1
2
Opt. both hands 8va
rit.

The Trees of the Field

STEFFI GEISER RUBIN
Based on Isaiah 55:12

STUART DAUERMANN
Arr. by Teresa Wilhelmi

trees of the field will clap their hands. The trees of the field will
clap their hands. The trees of the field will clap their hands While
Opt. Fine
you go out with joy.
You shall go out with joy and be led forth with peace. The
moun- tains and the hills will break forth be - fore you. There'll be

shouts of joy, and all the trees of the field will clap, will clap their
hands. And all the trees of the field will clap their hands. The
trees of the field will clap their hands. The trees of the field will
clap their hands While you go out with joy.
2 1 2 3 1 2 1
2
5

Holy, Holy, Holy! Lord God Almighty

REGINALD HEBER

JOHN B. DYKES
Arr. by Teresa Wilhelmi

rit.
a tempo
f
3. Holy, holy, holy!
Lord God Almighty!
All Thy works shall praise Thy name in
earth, and sky, and sea.
Holy, holy, holy!
merciful and
mighty!
God in three Persons, blessed Trinity!
8va

Holy, Holy

J. O.

JIMMY OWENS
Arr. by Teresa Wilhelmi

1. Ho - ly, ho - ly, ho - ly, ho - ly, Ho - ly, ho - ly,
2. Gra - cious Fa - ther, gra - cious Fa - ther, We're so blest to be Your
3. Pre - cious Je - sus, pre - cious Je - sus, We're so glad that You've re -
Lord God Al - might - y; And we lift our hearts be - fore You as a
chil - dren, gra - cious Fa - ther; And we lift our heads be - fore You as a
deemed us, pre - cious Je - sus; And we lift our hands be - fore You as a
If using the arrangement as a piano solo, omit this repeat.
to - ken of our love, Ho - ly, ho - ly, ho - ly, ho - ly.
to - ken of our love, Gra - cious Fa - ther, gra - cious Fa - ther.
to - ken of our love, Pre - cious Je - sus, pre - cious Je - sus.

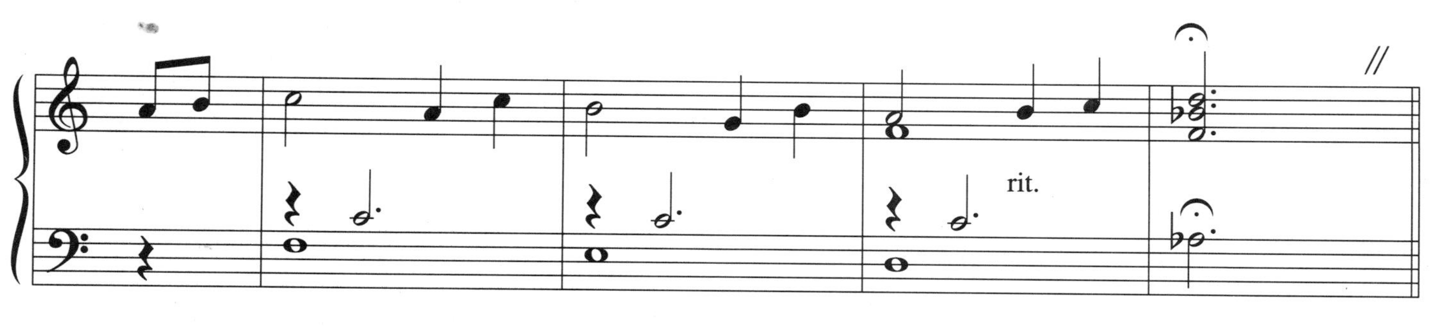
rit.

4. Ho - ly Spir - it, Ho - ly Spir - it, Come and fill our hearts a - new, Ho - ly

Spir - it; And we lift our voice be - fore You as a to - ken of our love, Ho - ly

Opt. tag
rit.
Spir - it, Ho - ly Spir - it.

Because of Who You Are

B. F.

BOB FARRELL and BILLY SMILEY
Arr. by Teresa Wilhelmi

a tempo
Lord, I praise You be-cause of who You are, Not be -
cause of all the might-y things You've done. Lord, I wor - ship You be-cause of
who You are; You're all the rea-son that I need to voice my praise, Be-cause of who You
are.
rit.

Great Is the Lord

M. W. S. and D. D. S.

MICHAEL W. and DEBORAH D. SMITH
Arr. by Teresa Wilhelmi

Great is the Lord; He is ho - ly and just. By His pow - er we trust in His
Great is the Lord; He is faith - ful and true. By His mer - cy He proves He is
love.
love.
Great is the Lord and wor - thy of glo - ry!
(D.S.) Great are You, Lord, and wor - thy of glo - ry!

Great is the Lord and wor- thy of praise! Great is the Lord! Now
Great are You, Lord, and wor- thy of praise! Great are You Lord! I
lift up your voice; now lift up your voice: Great is the
lift up my voice; I lift up my voice: Great are You,
Lord! Great is the
Lord! Great are You,
1
D. S.
2
Lord!
Lord!

This Is My Father's World

MALTBIE D. BABCOCK

FRANKLIN L. SHEPPARD
Arr. by Teresa Wilhelmi

If using the arrangement as a piano solo, omit this repeat.
skies and seas– His hand the won - ders wrought.
hear Him pass; He speaks to me ev - 'ry - where.
rit.
a tempo
3. This is my Fa - ther's world. O let me ne'er for -
get That tho' the wrong seems oft so strong, God is the Rul - er
yet. This is my Fa - ther's world. The bat - tle is not done; Je -
rit.
sus, who died, shall be sat - is - fied, And earth and heav'n be one.

Make Me a Servant

K. W.

KELLY WILLARD
Arr. by Teresa Wilhelmi

8va

Be Thou My Vision

TRADITIONAL IRISH HYMN, tr. by Mary E. Byrne

TRADITIONAL IRISH MELODY
Arr. by Teresa Wilhelmi

Flowing, with much expression
3
1. Be Thou my Vi - sion, O Lord of my heart; Naught be all else to me,
2. Be Thou my Wis - dom, and Thou my true Word; I ev - er with Thee and
save that Thou art– Thou my best thought, by day or by night,
Thou with me, Lord; Thou my great Fa - ther, I Thy true son,
If using the arrangement as a piano solo, omit this repeat.
Wak - ing or sleep - ing, Thy pres - ence my light.
Thou in me dwell - ing, and I with Thee one.

rall.
a tempo
3. Rich - es I
heed not, nor man's emp - ty praise,
Thou mine in - her - i - tance,
now and al - ways;
Thou and Thou on - ly, first in my
rall.
a tempo
heart,
High King of Heav - en, my Trea - sure Thou art.
rit.
3
8va

Where the Spirit of the Lord Is

S. R. A.

STEPHEN R. ADAMS
Arr. by Teresa Wilhelmi

Where the Spir- it of the
Lord is, there is peace; Where the Spir- it of the Lord is,
there is love. There is com-fort in life's dark - est hour. There is light and life; there is
help and pow-er in the Spir- it, in the Spir- it of the Lord.

Opt. Fine

rit.

I Live!

R. C.

RICH COOK
Arr. by Teresa Wilhelmi

In one
I
live, I live be - cause He is ris - en; I live, I
live, I live be - cause He is ris - en; I live, I
1
2
live with pow'r o - ver sin. I
live to wor - ship Him. Thank You, Je -
sus! Thank You, Je - sus! Be - cause You're a - live, be -
Opt. Fine
cause You're a - live, Be - cause You're a - live, I live!

slight rit.
3
a tempo
1
2
rit.

I Exalt Thee

P. S., Jr.

PETE SANCHEZ, Jr.
Arr. by Teresa Wilhelmi

gods.
I ex - alt Thee!
I ex - alt Thee!
I ex -
alt Thee,
O Lord!
1
2
I ex-
Lord!
Opt. Fine
rit.
a tempo

3
3
3
3
1
2
rit.

I Am Ready

T. P.

TWILA PARIS
Arr. by Teresa Wilhelmi

read - y now to be fi - nal - ly
1
me.
2
I am faith - ful - ly,
wil- ling - ly me.
Opt. Fine
Ped.

Ped.

Joyful, Joyful, We Adore Thee

3. Mor-tals join the might-y cho-rus Which the morn-ing
stars be-gan. Fa-ther-love is reign-ing o'er us; Broth-er-love binds
man to man. Ev-er sing-ing, march we on-ward, Vic-tors in the midst of strife.
rit.
Joy-ful mu-sic leads us sun-ward In the tri-umph song of life!

I Will Bless the Lord

F. H.

FRANK HERNANDEZ
Arr. by Teresa Wilhelmi

I
will
bless
the
Lord
and
give
Him
glo
-
ry.
Oh,
I
will
bless
His
name
and
give
Him
glo
-
ry.
The
2nd time to Coda

Lord is gra - cious and mer - ci - ful, Great in
kind - ness and good to all. The Lord is righ - teous in
all His ways; Bless the Lord and give Him
D.S. al Coda
CODA
praise. ry.

O the Deep, Deep Love of Jesus

SAMUEL TREVOR FRANCIS

THOMAS J. WILLIAMS, 1890
Arr. by Teresa Wilhelmi

Opt. Fine
rest a - bove.
2. O the deep, deep
How He lov - eth,
love of Je - sus–
ev - er lov - eth,
Spread His praise from shore to
Chang - eth nev - er, nev - er -
shore!
more;
How He watch - es o'er His loved ones, Died to call them
all His own;
How for them He in - ter - ced - eth,
Watch - eth o'er them from the throne.
Opt. tag
rit.

Lord, We Praise You

O. S.

OTIS SKILLINGS
Arr. by Teresa Wilhelmi

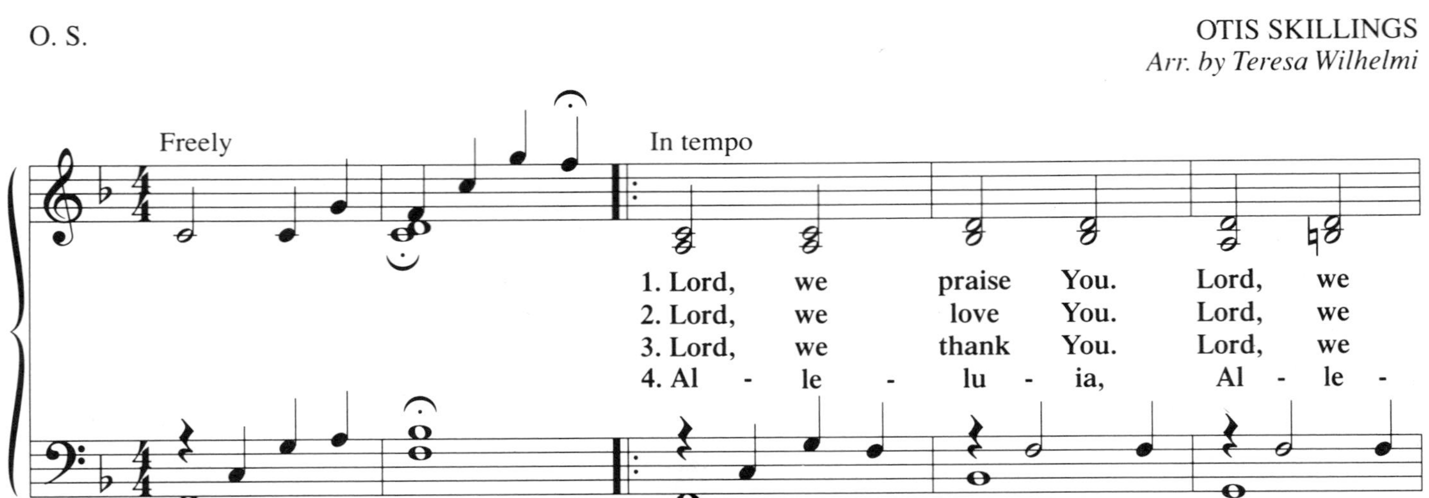
Freely
In tempo
1. Lord, we praise You. Lord, we
2. Lord, we love You. Lord, we
3. Lord, we thank You. Lord, we
4. Al - le - lu - ia, Al - le -

If using the arrangement as a piano solo, omit this repeat.
praise You. Lord, we praise You. We praise You, Lord.
love You. Lord, we love You. We love You, Lord.
thank You. Lord, we thank You. We thank You, Lord.
lu - ia, Al - le - lu - ia, We give You praise.

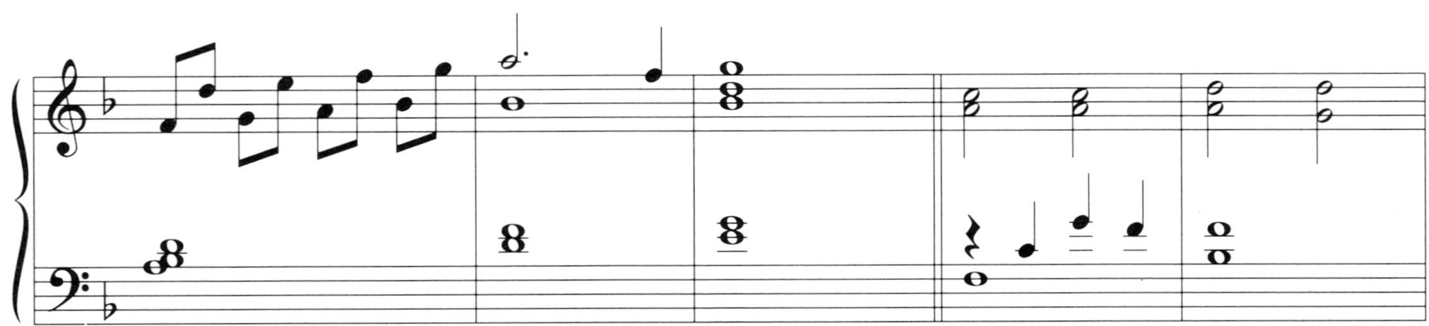

rall.
a tempo
pp
cresc. little by little
mp
decresc.
rit.
p

All Hail King Jesus

D. M.

DAVE MOODY
Arr. by Teresa Wilhelmi

All hail King Jesus. All hail Emmanuel, King of Kings, Lord of Lords, Bright Morning Star. And thro'-

out e - ter - ni - ty, I'll sing His prais - es, And I'll

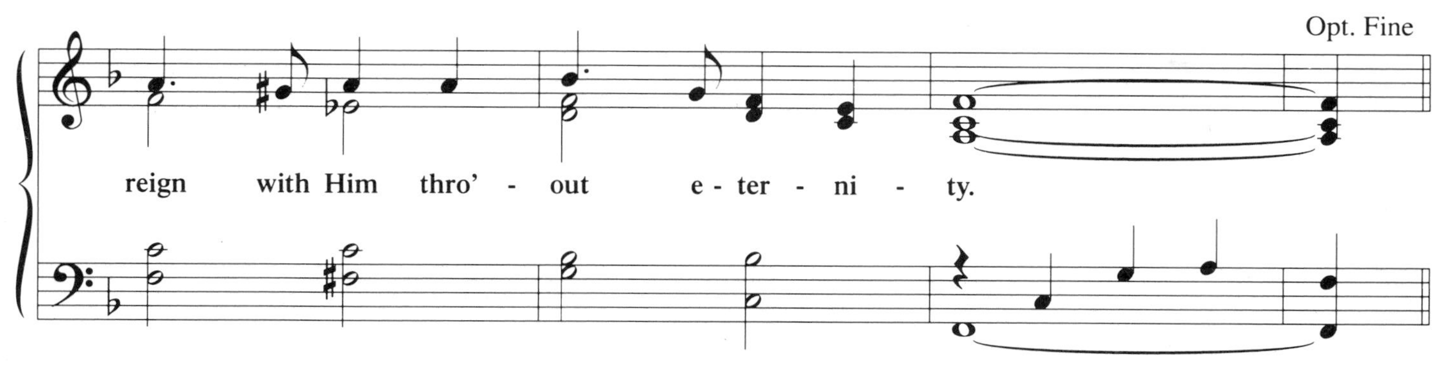
Opt. Fine
reign with Him thro' - out e - ter - ni - ty.

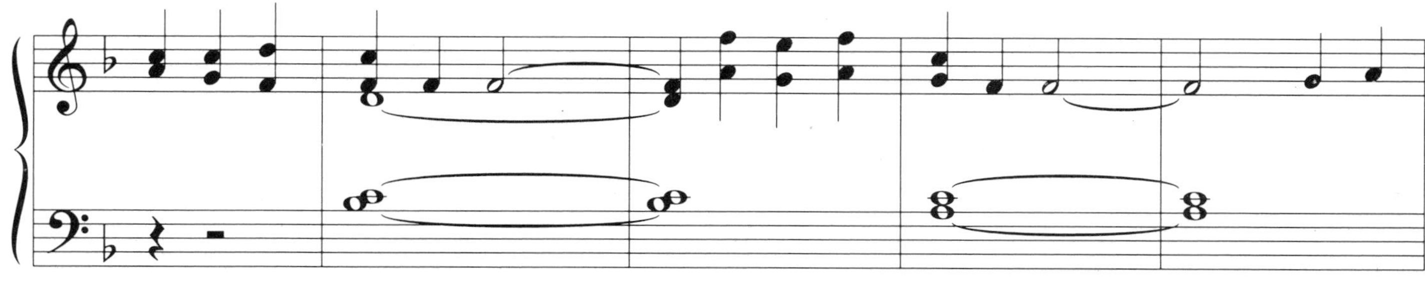

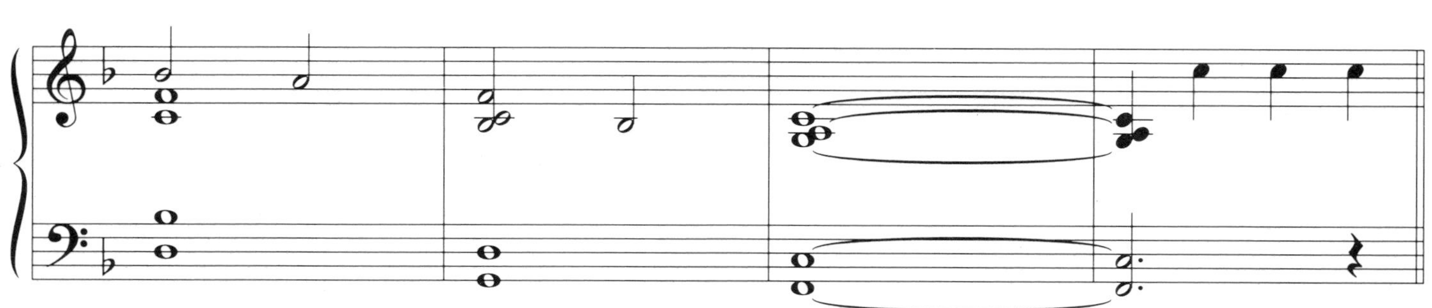

3
3
Opt. tag

He Is Exalted

T. P.

TWILA PARIS
Arr. by Teresa Wilhelmi

In two
He is ex-alt-ed, the King is ex-alt-ed on
high; I will praise Him.
He is ex-alt-ed, for - ev-er ex-alt-ed, and
I will praise His name!
He is the Lord; for - ev - er His truth shall reign.

Heav - en and earth re - joice in His ho - ly name.
Opt. Fine
He is ex - alt - ed, the King is ex - alt - ed on high.

Ped.

Jesus, Lord to Me

G. McS. and G. N.

GARY McSPADDEN and GREG NELSON
Arr. by Teresa Wilhelmi